D0934488

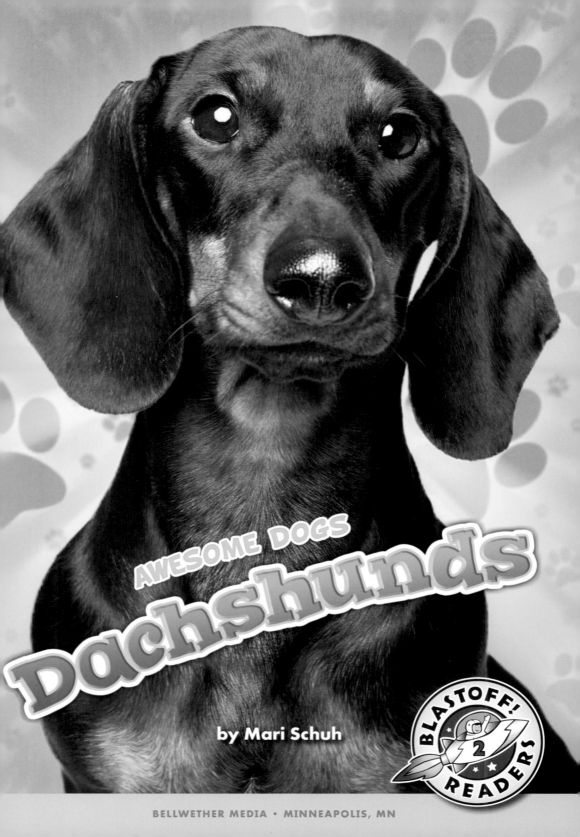

AWESOME DOGS

Dachshunds

by Mari Schuh

BLASTOFF!
2
READERS

BELLWETHER MEDIA • MINNEAPOLIS, MN

Note to Librarians, Teachers, and Parents:

Blastoff! Readers are carefully developed by literacy experts and combine standards-based content with developmentally appropriate text.

Level 1 provides the most support through repetition of high-frequency words, light text, predictable sentence patterns, and strong visual support.

Level 2 offers early readers a bit more challenge through varied simple sentences, increased text load, and less repetition of high-frequency words.

Level 3 advances early-fluent readers toward fluency through increased text and concept load, less reliance on visuals, longer sentences, and more literary language.

Level 4 builds reading stamina by providing more text per page, increased use of punctuation, greater variation in sentence patterns, and increasingly challenging vocabulary.

Level 5 encourages children to move from "learning to read" to "reading to learn" by providing even more text, varied writing styles, and less familiar topics.

Whichever book is right for your reader, Blastoff! Readers are the perfect books to build confidence and encourage a love of reading that will last a lifetime!

This edition first published in 2016 by Bellwether Media, Inc.

No part of this publication may be reproduced in whole or in part without written permission of the publisher. For information regarding permission, write to Bellwether Media, Inc., Attention: Permissions Department, 5357 Penn Avenue South, Minneapolis, MN 55419.

Library of Congress Cataloging-in-Publication Data

Schuh, Mari C., 1975- author.
  Dachshunds / by Mari Schuh.
     pages cm. – (Blastoff! Readers. Awesome Dogs)
  Summary: "Relevant images match informative text in this introduction to dachshunds. Intended for students in kindergarten through third grade"– Provided by publisher.
  Audience: Ages 5-8
  Audience: K to grade 3
  Includes bibliographical references and index.
  ISBN 978-1-62617-238-8 (hardcover: alk. paper)
  1. Dachshunds–Juvenile literature. 2. Dogs–Juvenile literature. I. Title.
  SF429.D25S368 2016
  636.753'8–dc23
                      2015008703

Printed in the United States of America, North Mankato, MN.

Table of Contents

What Are Dachshunds?

Dachshunds are a **unique** dog **breed**. They have long bodies and short, stubby legs.

They are also called
wiener dogs or hot dogs.

Dachshunds come in two sizes. Standard dachshunds weigh 16 to 32 pounds (7 to 15 kilograms).

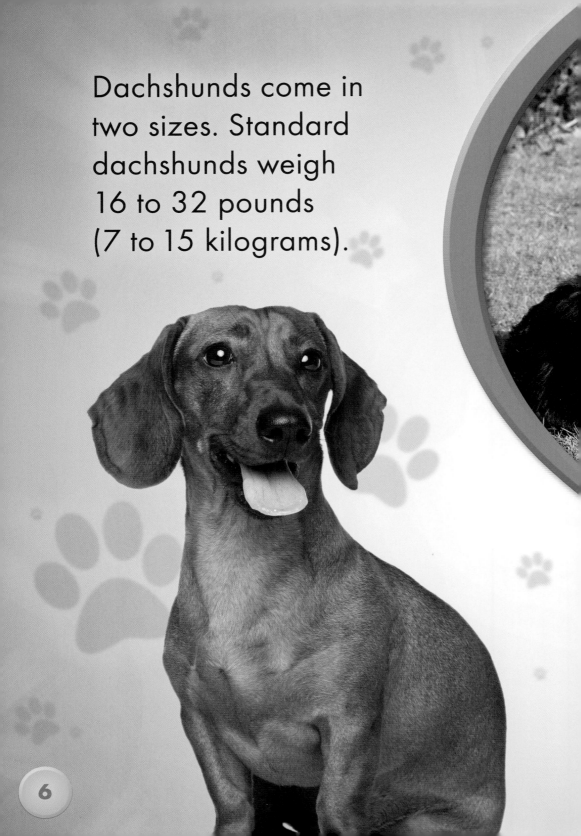

Miniature dachshunds weigh
under 11 pounds (5 kilograms).

Coats and Colors

Dachshunds have three **coat** types. They can be smooth, long-haired, or wire-haired.

Dachshund Coats

smooth   long-haired   wire-haired

Wire-haired dachshunds have stiff, thick hairs.

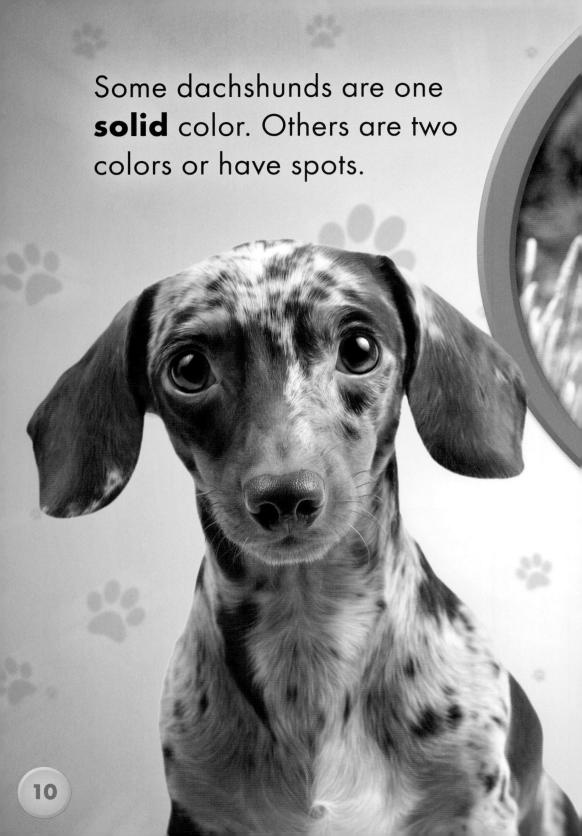

Some dachshunds are one **solid** color. Others are two colors or have spots.

Dachshund coats are most often black and tan or reddish brown.

History of Dachshunds

Dachshunds came from Germany more than 500 years ago. They were **bred** to be brave hunting dogs.

Germany

N
W · E
S

These dogs first hunted badgers.
The name *dachshund* is German
for "badger dog."

The dogs dug holes to find animals. Strong legs and large paws helped them dig.

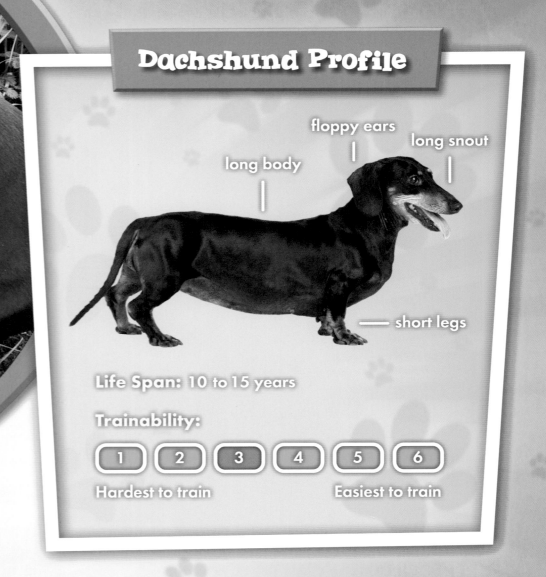

Dachshund Profile

long body

floppy ears

long snout

short legs

Life Span: 10 to 15 years

Trainability:

| 1 | 2 | 3 | 4 | 5 | 6 |

Hardest to train

Easiest to train

A dachshund's long body fit into animal **burrows**. Its loud bark called to hunters.

A strong sense of smell
helped the dachshund
hunt. Its long **snout**
caught **scents**.

Dachshunds are now in the **American Kennel Club**. They join other hunters in the **Hound Group**.

Dachshunds do not let their small size stop them.

They are **curious** and full of energy. But they can also be **stubborn**.

Some dachshunds work as **therapy dogs**. They visit hospitals and schools.

These long dogs also make loving and lively pets!

Glossary

American Kennel Club—an organization that keeps track of dog breeds in the United States

bred—purposely mated two dogs to make puppies with certain qualities

breed—a type of dog

burrows—holes or tunnels that some animals dig in the ground

coat—the hair or fur covering an animal

curious—interested or excited to learn or know about something

Hound Group—a group of dog breeds that often have a history of hunting

scents—odors and smells

snout—a dog's nose

solid—one color

stubborn—wanting to have your way or refusing to change

therapy dogs—dogs that comfort people who are sick, hurt, or have a disability

unique—one of a kind

To Learn More

AT THE LIBRARY
Beal, Abigail. *I Love My Dachshund*. New York, N.Y.: PowerKids Press, 2011.

George, Charles and Linda. *Dachshund*. New York, N.Y.: Children's Press, 2010.

Leaf, Munro. *Noodle*. New York, N.Y.: Arthur A. Levine Books, 2006.

ON THE WEB
Learning more about dachshunds is as easy as 1, 2, 3.

1. Go to www.factsurfer.com.

2. Enter "dachshunds" into the search box.

3. Click the "Surf" button and you will see a list of related web sites.

With factsurfer.com, finding more information is just a click away.

Index

The images in this book are reproduced through the courtesy of: jagodka, front cover, pp. 5, 6; Mark Raycroft/ Kimball Stock, p. 4; FLPA, p. 7; Klein-Hubert/ Kimball Stock, p. 8; Eric Isselee, p. 9 (left, center); Erik Lam, p. 9 (right); Ekaterina Brusnika, p. 10; Juniors/ SuperStock, p. 11; eans, p. 12; Karl Friedrich Deiker/ Wikipedia, p. 13; Deposit Photos/ Glow Images, p. 14; Alexia Khruscheva, p. 15; somamix1, p. 16; Tierfotoagentur/ Alamy, p. 17; Anna Hudorozkova, p. 18; H Schmidt-Roeger/ Age Fotostock, p. 19; Miller, Michele/ZUMA Press/ Newscom, p. 20; YinYang, p. 21.